Praise for EARTH & EROS

"In a world of distraction and grief, *Earth & Eros* returns us to our own wise senses. All praise to the lyrical writing, the gorgeous photographs: testimony to the power of embodied delight."

–Christian McEwen, author of *World Enough & Time: On Creativity and Slowing Down* and *Sparks from the Anvil: The Smith College Poetry Interviews*

"A masterpiece of discovery and juxtaposition. Reading the beautiful and thought-provoking text alongside photos as glossy and dense as reality feels like waking up, like remembering."

–Kim Stanley Robinson, Hugo and Nebula Award–winning author of *Forty Signs of Rain, 2312,* and *Aurora*

"A book of vivid voices and lush images to be savored and cherished. *Earth & Eros* offers a way to re-root ourselves back into our own bodies, the Earth, and our wildly alive and sensual natures."

–Mary Reynolds Thompson, author of *Reclaiming the Wild Soul* and *Embrace Your Inner Wild*

"An exceptional resource and an artistic treasure, *Earth & Eros* reminds us that the planet is a very sexy place. Reading these luscious poems and prose passages and staring into Bruce Hodge's stunning photos arouses an awareness of the intimacy between body, language, art, and nature."

–Henry Hughes, author of *Men Holding Eggs* (winner of the Oregon Book Award) and *Moist Meridian*

"This glorious book of hours makes the land the object of our meditation and desire. Accompanying sensuous images of nature are passages about living from a larger love—from an eros that extends from cell to body to family to community to this blue ball of earth, with all its wildness and wonder. This is the work of our age, and of the ages."

–Valerie Andrews, author of A Passion for This Earth

"Dominant and domineering Western culture has built its fortress on Logos. We have lost the wisdom that might situate its threads within the greater story lines of Mythos. Lorraine Anderson's anthology weaves such connections back to touch through Eros. She helps us to re-member what has been dis-membered."

–Alastair McIntosh, author of Soil and Soul and Hell and High Water

"Earth & Eros is a lovely, stirring, and significant book. It is a gift to those who love the reeling world. Because we are joined to the Earth, rejoicing in our deep connection to its tides, we are called to defend it—fiercely, faithfully, for all time."

–Kathleen Dean Moore, author of Wild Comfort and Great Tide Rising

EARTH & EROS
A Celebration in Words and Photographs

EARTH & EROS

A Celebration in Words and Photographs

compiled by **Lorraine Anderson**   photographs by **Bruce Hodge**
foreword by **Robert Michael Pyle**

White Cloud Press
Ashland, Oregon

A portion of the proceeds from this book will go to TreeSisters (treesisters.org), working toward empowering women and swiftly reforesting our world.

White Cloud Press titles may be purchased for educational, business, or sales promotional use. For information, please write:

Special Market Department
White Cloud Press
PO Box 3400, Ashland, OR 97520
Website: www.whitecloudpress.com

Cover and interior design by Christy Collins, C Book Services
Printed in South Korea

15 16 17 18 19 20   10 9 8 7 6 5 4 3 2 1

Library of Congress Cataloging-in-Publication Data

Earth & Eros : a celebration in words and photographs / compiled by Lorraine Anderson ; photographs by Bruce Hodge ; foreword by Robert Michael Pyle.

     pages cm
 Includes bibliographical references and index.
 ISBN 978-1-940468-28-0 (paperback)
1. Nature--Literary collections. 2. Nature photography. I. Anderson, Lorraine, 1952- II. Hodge, Bruce.
PS509.N3E23 2015
810.8'036--dc23
                          2015032114

A little too abstract, a little too wise,
It is time for us to kiss the earth again . . .
ROBINSON JEFFERS, FROM "RETURN"

If we survive as a species, it will have nothing to do with what we've invented, developed or manufactured, but everything to do with what we know in our deep cores about being good mammals.
BROOKE WILLIAMS, FROM *HALF LIVES*

CONTENTS

THE EARTH WHISPERS AND CROONS

One time, for me, it was a Roman snail on the South Downs of Sussex. The apple-sized mollusk spread the slick flesh of its foot over my middle finger as if I were its parthenogenetic partner. Labial, febrile, that slippery lick of my flesh gave me tingles until a sharp jab let me know that the escargot had actually fired its love dart right into my skin.

Another time, it was among the monarchs in Michoacán, at 10,000 feet. After a great, freezing storm, millions lay dead in windrows and drifts beneath the oyamel firs where the survivors still hung. Sick in my chest from city smog, in my heart from all those dead, I lay back into that cinnamon sediment and felt myself getting well. Turning over, I embraced the blanket of butterflies like a featherbed, arms, thighs, face, all feathered in wings, stroked by scales.

There was the night of warm waters, salt Gulf waters that I couldn't tell from skin, when the noctiluca bloomed. All over, around, above me their green sparks sparked, between my legs, between my toes, through my hair, the chartreuse shimmers flickered and leaped. Walking through them was a shimmy in emerald sequins.

And the day of the desert sycamores, up a wet chute coming out of the Chiricahuas. I had no choice but to crawl out on that broad branch of the green-barked sycamore. It was not my decision to fondle its round knobs, to cleave to its sinuous limbs, to caress its mossy clefts.

I won't say they weren't sexy, that tree, that shimmy, that lay-me-down in butterflies, that snail. And the times with a lover! Coupling in dry leaves or awkward sand, on ash tree bough, in rough surf. Pressing flowers with our bodies on a coastal heath in Dorset—pink heather, early purple orchids, bog asphodel . . . but, through grace, not gorse.

There is nothing symbolic about any of this. Any more than D. H. Lawrence's lessons of catkins and figs—their long danglers, their purple slits—are merely metaphors. They are their own real things. And earth *is* eros. Anyone who supposes otherwise, or who still labors under the tired notion that nature and people are twain, need only read on. The poems and prose in this beguiling (and let's face it, very sexy) book will lead you into pathways of sensual connection you may have suppressed, or forgotten, or once celebrated and long to celebrate again.

Lorraine Anderson has artfully selected writing both spiritual and physical (there being no clear difference between the two, as far as I can see); pieces of deep thoughtfulness and others heedless in the way of thought, in favor of passion; poems plain and rhapsodic. Honeypie-in-the-sky, feet in the sticky mud, bone to flesh to water to rock. The extraordinarily varied authors represented here are each of them clearly in love with the world and all that makes it up. Paired with Bruce Hodge's blood-quickening images, they will leave you in no doubt that this same world has as much to give your body and heart as you are willing and open to receive.

For why, after all, are salacious jokes and sexual language referred to as earthy? Because there is no randier, lustier lover than the earth, is why. What better time than now for such a book, when this lover is in distress, and we are stoking her up beyond the boiling point? These days, when pollination is the hottest thing in conservation, shouldn't we recognize the essential sameness between our own desire and every other attraction: electron to proton, duck to drake, badger to humping badger, leaf to mould? As Pattiann Rogers says in "The Power of Toads," "Raindrops-finding-earth and coitus could very well / Be known here as one."

So be it. We lovers of literature and the land, and of one another, may rejoice in the knowledge that we are not alone in bringing our passion to the wind, the trees, the soil. As this book whispers and croons, the passion was already there to meet us.

ROBERT MICHAEL PYLE
GRAY'S RIVER, WASHINGTON

EROS AND THE NEW WORLD CRYING TO BE BORN

Eros. The irresistible siren of desire. The red cord of passion. The hunger that cries to be filled, the thirst that must be quenched. The mysterious force that propels every life form, pushing roses to bloom, hummingbirds to migrate, and salmon to swim upriver to spawn. The force of life seeking to fulfill itself, reaching, surging, expanding, unfolding. The life force that connects us to ourselves, to other humans, to all other living beings on the earth, and to the earth as a living being.

Eros encompasses our sensuality and sexuality, yes, but it embraces so much more—the deepest longings of body, heart, and soul, our deepest roots in earth. "Eros is the bond in the ecological communion within which we live. It is not primarily an emotion, a decision, or the result of an act of will. It is the mutuality linking cell to cell, animal to environment, without which we would not be," writes philosopher Sam Keen in *The Passionate Life*.

Eros in our world is most often narrowly understood as romantic and sexual love and lust between humans. Perhaps it is no coincidence that the earth is so often bent to our own uses rather than seen as an intimate partner to be loved, savored, and revered. Perhaps there is a relationship between our limited concept of eros and our narrow valuing of nature solely for the "resources" it provides. We have forgotten the intimate, erotic relationship between our bodies and the earth, and the consequences are all around us.

The body of the earth is under attack in ways large and small each day. Drilled, mined, blown up, bulldozed, injected, drained, bombed, burned, clear-cut, fracked, dumped on, drowned, its climate increasingly altered by the greenhouse gas products of human activity, the earth staggers under the burden of industrial abuse, and so do we. Life on earth is imperiled, along with what is wildest and truest and most potent in ourselves. Entranced by screens and devices, worshipping speed and efficiency, treating our bodies as machines to earn money, in denial about the increasingly urgent messages we are hearing from our biosphere, we are kept from full presence to our own deepest desires.

"Oh what a catastrophe, what a maiming of love when it was made a personal, merely personal feeling, taken away from the rising and the setting of the sun, and cut off from the magic connection of the solstice and the equinox! That is what is the matter with us. We are bleeding at the roots, because we are cut off from the earth and sun and stars," wrote novelist D. H. Lawrence. Is there a different way of inhabiting our bodies and the earth? Eros, the force of desire, says yes.

Stop and take a deep breath. Breathe the air down into your heart, into your pelvis, into your toes. Feel your body as the earth of you, as a part of the larger body of the earth; feel yourself as a wild creature connected to a wild longing for health, wholeness, communion. Experience your deepest cravings. Know that the well-being of the earth depends on your passionate pursuit of what you most deeply desire in your cells, which is life abundant and overflowing.

Eros is the only force strong enough to move us to imagine and create the new world that is crying to be born. This is my conviction. And so I have gathered voices that explore the erotic dimension of the human relationship to the earth. You will find here poems and prose pieces that weave together images of the natural world with the language of desire. These words celebrate a sensuality that honors the earth and flesh as sacred. They recognize what the philosopher Maurice Merleau-Ponty called "our erotic embrace with the flesh of the world." They acknowledge the erotic as a force of nature, channeled through the untamed land, the unpredictable elements, the unbridled emotions, the unruly body.

The accompanying photographs reveal the sensual beauty of the planet we inhabit, our larger body. They call us to recognize the deep, freely available wellspring of pleasure, satisfaction, and fullness we can drink from whenever we choose to pay attention. Simply by opening our senses and feeling ourselves to be part of the natural world around us, we can begin to heal, to regain wholeness, to take communion.

Let this book open your eyes to the possibilities for deep pleasure everywhere around you. Read it out loud to yourself, to your lover. Let the words inspire you to infuse your wild, precious life with the primal gifts of love offered by the earth and to honor the earth in all your actions.

LORRAINE ANDERSON
CORVALLIS, OREGON

DESIRE

"Don't want too much," the voices warned.

No. Want. Want life.
Want this fragile oasis of a galaxy to flourish.
Want fertility, want seasons, want this spectacular array of creatures,
this brilliant balance of need.

Want it. Want it all.
Desire. Welcome her raging power.
May her strength course through us.
Desire, she is life. Desire life.
Allow ourselves to desire life, to want this sweetness so passionately,
that we live for it.

—ELLEN BASS, FROM "LIVE FOR IT"

We have been raised to fear the *yes* within ourselves, our deepest cravings. . . .
But when we begin to live from within outward, in touch with the power of the
erotic within ourselves, and allowing that power to inform and illuminate our
actions upon the world around us, then we begin to be responsible to ourselves
in the deepest sense.

–AUDRE LORDE, FROM "USES OF THE EROTIC: THE EROTIC AS POWER"

4

I believe in the flesh and the appetites,
Seeing, hearing, feeling, are miracles, and each part and tag of me is a miracle.

Divine am I inside and out, and I make holy whatever I touch or am touched from,
The scent of these arm-pits aroma finer than prayer,
This head more than churches, bibles, and all the creeds.

If I worship one thing more than another it shall be the spread of my own body,
    or any part of it,
Translucent mould of me it shall be you!
Shaded ledges and rests it shall be you!
Firm masculine colter it shall be you!
Whatever goes to the tilth of me it shall be you!
You my rich blood! your milky stream pale strippings of my life!

Breast that presses against other breasts it shall be you!
My brain it shall be your occult convolutions!
Root of washed sweet-flag! timorous pond-snipe! nest of guarded duplicate eggs!
    it shall be you!
Mixed tussled hay of head, beard, brawn, it shall be you!
Trickling sap of maple, fibre of manly wheat, it shall be you!
Sun so generous it shall be you!
Vapors lighting and shading my face it shall be you!
You sweaty brooks and dews it shall be you!
Winds whose soft-tickling genitals rub against me it shall be you!
Broad muscular fields, branches of live oak, loving lounger in my winding paths,
    it shall be you!
Hands I have taken, face I have kissed, mortal I have ever touched, it shall be you.

–WALT WHITMAN, FROM SECTION 24 OF "SONG OF MYSELF"

Children want to touch everything, to smell the flowers, taste the leaves, dangle their feet in the water, pick apart the scat, carry home the bones. Sometimes I am impatient about this desire for direct contact. "Have respect!" I want to say. But in the end I hold my tongue, knowing they pay their respects by making sensual contact with the world. "The opposite of love," a friend reminds me, "is not hatred, but indifference."

–PAUL GRUCHOW, FROM GRASS ROOTS: THE UNIVERSE OF HOME

O world, I cannot hold thee close enough!
Thy winds, thy wide grey skies!
Thy mists, that roll and rise!
Thy woods, this autumn day, that ache and sag
And all but cry with colour! That gaunt crag
To crush! To lift the lean of that black bluff!
World, World, I cannot get thee close enough!

Long have I known a glory in it all,
But never knew I this;
Here such a passion is
As stretcheth me apart,—Lord, I do fear
Thou'st made the world too beautiful this year;
My soul is all but out of me,—let fall
No burning leaf; prithee, let no bird call.

–Edna St. Vincent Millay, "God's World"

The apple on its bough is her desire,—
Shining suspension, mimic of the sun.
The bough has caught her breath up, and her voice,
Dumbly articulate in the slant and rise
Of branch on branch above her, blurs her eyes.
She is prisoner of the tree and its green fingers.

And so she comes to dream herself the tree,
The wind possessing her, weaving her young veins,
Holding her to the sky and its quick blue,
Drowning the fever of her hands in sunlight.
She has no memory, nor fear, nor hope
Beyond the grass and shadows at her feet.

–HART CRANE, "GARDEN ABSTRACT"

It was a spring afternoon in West Florida. Janie had spent most of the day under a blossoming pear tree in the back-yard. She had been spending every minute that she could steal from her chores under that tree for the last three days. That was to say, ever since the first tiny bloom had opened. It had called her to come and gaze on a mystery. From barren brown stems to glistening leaf-buds; from the leaf-buds to snowy virginity of bloom. It stirred her tremendously. How? Why? It was like a flute song forgotten in another existence and remembered again. What? How? Why? This singing she heard that had nothing to do with her ears. The rose of the world was breathing out smell. It followed her through all her waking moments and caressed her in her sleep. It connected itself with other vaguely felt matters that had struck her outside observation and buried themselves in her flesh. Now they emerged and quested about her consciousness.

She was stretched on her back beneath the pear tree soaking in the alto chant of the visiting bees, the gold of the sun and the panting breath of the breeze when the inaudible voice of it all came to her. She saw a dust-bearing bee sink into the sanctum of a bloom; the thousand sister-calyxes arch to meet the love embrace and the ecstatic shiver of the tree from root to tiniest branch creaming in every blossom and frothing with delight. So this was a marriage! She had been summoned to behold a revelation. Then Janie felt a pain remorseless sweet that left her limp and languid.

After a while she got up from where she was and went over the little garden field entire. She was seeking confirmation of the voice and vision, and everywhere she found and acknowledged answers. A personal answer for all other creations except herself. She felt an answer seeking her, but where? When? How? She found herself at the kitchen door and stumbled inside. In the air of the room were flies tumbling and singing, marrying and giving in marriage. When she reached the narrow hallway she was reminded that her grandmother was home with a sick headache. She was lying across the bed asleep so Janie tipped on out of the front door. Oh to be a pear tree—*any* tree in bloom! With kissing bees singing of the beginning of the world! She was sixteen. She had glossy leaves and bursting buds and she wanted to struggle with life but it seemed to elude her. Where were the singing bees for her? Nothing on the place nor in her grandma's house answered her. She searched as much of the world as she could from the top of the front steps and then went on down to the front gate and leaned over to gaze up and down the road. Looking, waiting, breathing short with impatience. Waiting for the world to be made.

–ZORA NEALE HURSTON, FROM *THEIR EYES WERE WATCHING GOD*

the geography of love is terra infirma

it is a paper boat
navigated by mates
with stars in their eyes

cartographers of the fiery unknown

it is the woman's sure hand
at the helm of twilight, the salt
compass of her desire

the map of longing is at the edge
of two distant bodies

it is the rain that launches thirst
it is the palm leaf floating on waters
far from shore

the secret passage into the interior
is in my intemperate estuary

the sweet and languorous flowering
is in the caliber of your hands

the circular motion of our journeying
is the radius of sky and sea, deep
    territories we name
    after ourselves

–ANITA ENDREZZE, "THE MAPMAKER'S DAUGHTER"

O ye frogs and fevers, ye coots and constellations, the fisher-girl was the loveliest of lovely sights! On the sunbaked boulder, on green moss she lay, the quicksilver trout, rose-hued and stippled, glimmering by her side, glistening by her side, a pale, paltry thing by her gleaming side. As she ran a slender finger through the moss, over the stone, along the wretched fish, only Heaven and myself knew the pain that I was in. And when at last I remembered to breathe, that breath came, that breath went, with a fall and rise of rose-tipped breasts. Birds flew, crickets sang, stone and river spoke together in the shallow, and her music low and lovely and the beauty of her body and the wind's soft singing and the beauty of her body O the beauty of her body beat upon me like a storm. Ah, what became of my mother's boy as he watched beside the river? What became of her fisher-son gazing on the gleaming girl?

–DAVID JAMES DUNCAN, FROM THE RIVER WHY

I remember falling a few steps behind on the path, purposely; I wanted to watch him take long strides up the hillside I love along the nearly invisible trails of deer and antelope. His shoulders were broad and steady, and each step seemed effortless. I took a deep breath—the air was filled with the redolence of sagebrush after a thunderstorm. I felt flooded with desire.

Now, in a city I don't love, I am staring into a puddle, but all I see is a muddled reflection of my face framed by waterlogged trees and power lines. I feel nothing spectacular.

I lift my gaze and continue walking. Unexpectedly, I catch a whiff of sagebrush, pungent and sensuous, and I pause to look around. A sagebrush sits stranded, awkwardly, just outside a neighbor's fence bordering their lush green yard. Bending over, I close my eyes and inhale deeply, hoping for the same overwhelming outpouring of love and desire I once experienced. Nothing.

I want to be surrounded by it, vulnerable in it. I scan the city block to make sure no one is watching, and then I sprawl out in the wood chips next to the sagebrush and close my eyes again, inhaling deeply—and I think of the high desert hillside: the sunset after the thunderstorm, the view over the rocky canyon, the stream tumbling down toward the valley I call home, the broad shoulders and tangle of trails, and his sagebrush-scented fingers brushing a wisp of hair out of my face. It's fleeting, but if only for a moment, I am satiated.

—SARA J. CALL IHRIE, FROM "DESERT IN THREE ACTS"

16

In the whole of the universe there are only two, lover and Beloved.

–SUFI SAYING

My beloved spoke and said unto me, "Rise up, my love, my fair one,
    and come away.
For lo, the winter is past, the rain is over and gone.
The flowers appear on the earth; the time of the singing of birds is come,
    and the voice of the turtledove is heard in our land.
The fig tree putteth forth her green figs, and the vines with the tender grape
    give a good smell. Arise, my love, my fair one, and come away."

–Song of Solomon, 2:10–13 (21st Century King James Version)

Spring equinox the first suitor arrives.
Bloodcurrant lets down pink locks
for rufous hummingbird's needled kiss.
Fawn lilies open for churly bees. Hermit thrush twirl
lassos of seductive song into the chill breeze, punctuated
by the chipping sparrow's impatient call.

Striped bass shimmy together in streams,
orange-crowned warblers chuckle overhead,
cinnamon teal strut the pond, sandhill cranes pose regal
beside cattail posts, eyes out for a mate, while
osprey press into each other in free fall. The mole emerges
from her burrow, invites the drowsy to rise as I

in my crumpled gown and squirrel hair remember
that you, Love, return to me today as I blink
into the grinning sun. *Come soon.*

—AMY MINATO, "MATING SEASON"

The sap rises in the maple each spring after
the squeeze and release, squeeze and release
of winter. The spirit rises up into the face
of a shepherd, light shining on his clothes
and legs, on his sheep, on the ground and on
the stranger standing nearby. Bodies, light,
sap, our language. The body and the spirit.
Would God put himself into the body of a man
if what he wanted was to escape from the body?
What if God wanted the tree to blossom simply
because it would be covered with purple flowers
without leaves as I remember seeing in Nicaragua?
The raised arms of a shepherd, the light
lighter at the horizon of black hills. Moonlight
falling passionately on the stranger passing
the roadside gravestone. God trying to get down
to squeeze him in the dark. God cannot stop.

God is there and always sees the black ball
the crescent moon is holding. Sees the old tree
bent over by the storm in a field of wheat
lit up like the ocean. His grip is suffering,
revelation is the release. The sap rises up
in man and beasts, and in all things vegetable.
Plants and animals do it even better, kneeling
or celebrating or shining more immediately
than men do. But God loves us more, because
of the dread and seeking we contain. He loves
our lostness because it is by loneliness
and sacrifice, our body and soul together, that
the thing God is can exist. We are the stone
that is sacred. The way we make love with each
other is the collision that makes His face shine.
Makes the sap rise. God squeezes and relents
like winter ending, and the sap rising.

–LINDA GREGG, "THERE IS A SWEETNESS IN IT"

Usually we met, exchanged nonsequiturs while we fondled each other, and careened into bed unable to wait. Sex was always very good; a swollen stream coursing through a narrow canyon, sweeping everything before it, washing away the accumulated debris of winter, finally trickling out into the desert sand, spent. We were thankful to each other for the cleansing.

–SAM KEEN, FROM *THE PASSIONATE LIFE*

I think of you as
rain and I as dry earth cracked
beneath cloudless sky

–KALAMU YA SALAAM, "HAIKU #107"

If I were a female hummingbird perched still
And quiet on an upper myrtle branch
In the spring afternoon and if you were a male
Alone in the whole heavens before me, having parted
Yourself, for me, from cedar top and honeysuckle stem
And earth down, your body hovering in midair
Far away from jewelweed, thistle, and bee balm;

And if I watched how you fell, plummeting before me,
And how you rose again and fell, with such mastery
That I believed for a moment you were the sky
And the red-marked bird diving inside your circumference
Was just the physical revelation of the light's
Most perfect desire;

And if I saw your sweeping and sucking
Performance of swirling egg and semen in the air,
The weaving, twisting vision of red petal
And nectar and soaring rump, the rush of your wing
In its grand confusion of arcing and splitting
Created completely out of nothing just for me,

Then when you came down to me, I would call you
My own spinning bloom of ruby sage, my funnelling
Storm of sunlit sperm and pollen, my only breathless
Piece of scarlet sky, and I would bless the base
Of each of your feathers and touch the tine
Of string muscles binding your wings and taste
The odor of your glistening oils and hunt
The honey in your crimson flare
And I would take you and take you and take you
Deep into any kind of nest you ever wanted.

–PATTIANN ROGERS, "THE HUMMINGBIRD: A SEDUCTION"

26

Come up into the hills, O my young love. Return! O lost and by the wind grieved, ghost, come back again, as first I knew you in that timeless valley, where we shall feel ourselves anew, bedded on magic in the month of June. There was a place where all the sun went glistering in your hair, and from the hill we could have put a finger on a star.

–THOMAS WOLFE, FROM *LOOK HOMEWARD, ANGEL*

she held the stone wet from the river
so black and glimmering it could have been a dark star
they shouted down from last night's sky

a magpie semaphored through the green cottonwoods
calling complaints against their presence
while the river giggled past their feet like talkative wine
and the sun wrapped them tight in their yearning

—it's a jewel she said
i want you to have it

he took it from her with hands twining
water mingling on skin and rock like oilslick in the heat of day

the sky danced in her brown eyes and time stopped in his heart

–T. H. WATKINS, "THE RIVER STONE"

And then I asked him with my eyes to ask again yes and then he asked me
would I yes to say yes my mountain flower and first I put my arms around
him yes and drew him down to me so he could feel my breasts all perfume
yes and his heart was going like mad and yes I said yes I will Yes.

–James Joyce, from *Ulysses*

SENSUALITY

I understood that
our sensuality is grounded
in Nature, in Compassion
and in Grace.
This enables us to receive
gifts that lead to
everlasting life.
For I saw that in our sensuality
God is.
For God is never out of
the soul.

–JULIAN OF NORWICH, FROM MEDITATIONS WITH JULIAN OF NORWICH

"Jesus is our true Mother in whom we are endlessly
carried and out of whom we will never come."

–Julian of Norwich

    Christ's blood is green
        in the branches,
    blue in the violet.
        Her bright voice
    laughs in the night wind.
        The big nova swells
    in her breast.
        Christ suckles us
    with spring sap and
        spreads earth under our feet.

    O she loves us,
    feeds us, tricks us with her triple ways:
    calls us soul,
    calls us body, and spirit.
    Calls us to her bed.

    –M. C. Richards, "Deep Ecology"

34

Some years ago, when I had taken a job directing a writing program in St. Louis, Missouri, I often used color as a tonic. Regardless of the oasis-eyed student in my office, or the last itchlike whim of the secretary, or the fumings of the hysterically anxious chairman, I tried to arrive home at around the same time every evening, to watch the sunset from the large picture window in my living room, which overlooked Forest Park. Each night the sunset surged with purple pampas-grass plumes, and shot fuchsia rockets into the pink sky, then deepened through folded layers of peacock green to all the blues of India and a black across which clouds sometimes churned like alabaster dolls. The visual opium of the sunset was what I craved. Once, while eating a shrimp-and-avocado salad at the self-consciously stately faculty club, I found myself restless for the day to be over and all such tomblike encounters to pale, so I could drag my dinette-set chair up to the window and purge my senses with the pure color and visual tumult of the sunset. This happened again the next day in the coffee room, where I stood chatting with one of the literary historians, who always wore the drabbest camouflage colors and continued talking long after a point had been made. I set my facial muscles at "listening raptly," as she chuntered on about her specialty, the Caroline poets, but in my mind the sun was just beginning to set, a green glow was giving way to streaks of sulfur yellow, and a purple cloud train had begun staggering across the horizon. I was paying too much rent for my apartment, she explained. True, the apartment overlooked the park's changing seasons, had a picture window that captured the sunset every night, and was only a block away from a charming cobblestone area full of art galleries, antique stores, and ethnic restaurants. But this was all an *expense*, as she put it, with heavy emphasis on the second syllable, not just financial expense, but a too-extravagant experience of life. That evening, as I watched the sunset's pinwheels of apricot and mauve slowly explode into red ribbons, I thought: *The sensory misers will inherit the earth, but first they will make it not worth living on.*

When you consider something like death, after which (there being no news flash to the contrary) we may well go out like a candle flame, then it probably doesn't matter if we try too hard, are awkward sometimes, care for one another too deeply, are excessively curious about nature, are too open to experience, enjoy a nonstop expense of the senses in an effort to know life intimately and lovingly. It probably doesn't matter if, while trying to be modest and eager watchers of life's many spectacles, we sometimes look clumsy or get dirty or ask stupid questions or reveal our ignorance or say the wrong thing or light up with wonder like the children we all are. It probably doesn't matter if a passerby sees us dipping a finger into the moist pouches of dozens of lady's slippers to find out what bugs tend to fall into them, and thinks us a bit eccentric. Or a neighbor, fetching her mail, sees us standing in the cold with our own letters in one hand and a seismically red autumn leaf in the other, its color hitting our senses like a blow from a stun gun, as we stand with a huge grin, too paralyzed by the intricately veined gaudiness of the leaf to move.

–DIANE ACKERMAN, FROM *A NATURAL HISTORY OF THE SENSES*

For man, the vast marvel is to be alive. For man, as for flower and beast and bird, the supreme triumph is to be most vividly, most perfectly alive. Whatever the unborn and dead may know, they cannot know the beauty, the marvel of being alive in the flesh. The dead may look after the afterwards. But the magnificent here and now of life in the flesh is ours, and ours alone, and ours only for a time. We ought to dance with rapture that we should be alive and in the flesh, and part of the living, incarnate cosmos.

–D. H. LAWRENCE, FROM *APOCALYPSE*

Owning up to being an animal, a creature of the earth. Turning our animal senses to the sensible terrain: blending our skin with the rain-rippled surface of rivers, mingling our ears with the thunder and the thrumming of frogs, and our eyes with the molten sky. Feeling the polyrhythmic pulse of this place— this huge windswept body of water and stone. This vexed being in whose flesh we're entangled.

Becoming earth. Becoming animal. Becoming, in this manner, fully human.

–DAVID ABRAM, FROM BECOMING ANIMAL

Spring dusk. It is the blue of a smoking engine out there, and now, from the pond, the rippling sexual sobs of wood frogs, bullfrogs, the full-throated breathing of the deep night, begin. It is a song so powerful I lie upon the bed pressed into the waves. The air throbs, filled and running over with alluring Spanish *r*'s. This is the night in its entirety—leaves, grass, quaking air. The sound inhabits me, as if the dark passes into me, thrilling and complete. I walk out at midnight to stand within the tension as the moon shows, gleaming and porous, through the stanchions of pine.

Black stalls housing black horses, black grass, black trees, whir of black wings at the back of my head. Waking in the deep blackness, nursing a baby, is the most sensuous of animal tasks. All night I wake, feed our baby, sleep, wake again to the tiny body curled to me in the depth of that seething music.

–LOUISE ERDRICH, FROM *THE BLUE JAY'S DANCE*

Now, after all these years, I remember the conversation
        with a woman I loved
who casually mentioned that mushrooms reminded her
        of penises

(soft skin, musky smell, potentially dangerous)

though I cannot recall if the comparison fascinated
        or repelled her.
She left me soon after that conversation for
        another woman

(soft skin, musky smell, potentially dangerous)

And though I too have since fallen in love with
        and married
another woman, I often pause in the middle
        of lovemaking

(soft skin, musky smell, potentially dangerous)

to think about the fog-soaked forest into which
        we all travel
to think about the damp, dank earth into which
        we all plunge our hands

(soft skin, musky smell, potentially dangerous)

to search for water and spore and roof and loam
to search for water and room and root and home.

–SHERMAN ALEXIE, "THE ANATOMY OF MUSHROOMS"

It is the spring scent of the lilac, of roots and earth and lightning, the scent of rain on stone and the nectar bees gather from the wild flowering in the hollows on the wide bellies of the plains, or in the meadows that interrupt the sighing of the pine forests where the deer have come to graze, or in the passes between the volcanic mountain peaks. It is the scent of the evening or morning dew gathered on the tips of your fingers, in the inlets between your toes. It is the scent of these earthy things that brings this singer with nothing but his small drum of a voice.

It is nothing but these scents that bring this wandering mendicant here to wait, as one might wait by the side of a track for a train to come in the night. It is nothing but these scents that bring him here to spend his time worshipping, beneath moon and stars, the flesh that releases such pleasure into the darkness, happy to leave a song of his own here in the palms of your hands, in the curve of your thighs, in the arch of your spine, until the season when the corn is harvested and the vines are growing black.

–RANDY LUNDY, "AN EXPLANATION"

Eating the living germs of grasses
Eating the ova of large birds

      the fleshy sweetness packed
      around the sperm of swaying trees

The muscles of the flanks and thighs of
              soft-voiced cows
      the bounce in the lamb's leap
      the swish in the ox's tail

Eating roots grown swoll
      inside the soil

Drawing on life of living
      clustered points of light spun
          out of space
hidden in the grape.

Eating each other's seed
          eating
      ah, each other.

Kissing the lover in the mouth of bread:
      lip to lip.

–GARY SNYDER, "SONG OF THE TASTE"

44

As I lie beside you
my arm brushing your arm
I imagine how the feathery tongue
of the sapsucker curls
into a crevice in the grand fir.

And when my breasts pool
against your back I remember
how the soft toe pads of the tree frog
meld it to cedar bark.

Just when you roll toward me
a wave at sea skids bottom and its tip
releases into foam. And while I melt

a membrane slides over a pond turtle's eye
as it slips underwater making the world
now blurred and bluegreen
merged and magnified
tadpole, lily stalk, eel dart
rippled, polished, wet.

–AMY MINATO, "EROTICS"

Climbing alone all day long
In the blazing waste of spring snow,
I came down with the sunset's edge
To the highest meadow, green
In the cold mist of waterfalls,
To a cobweb of water
Woven with innumerable
Bright flowers of wild iris;
And saw far down our fire's smoke
Rising between the canyon walls,
A human thing in the empty mountains.
And as I stood on the stones
In the midst of whirling water,
The whirling iris perfume
Caught me in a vision of you
More real than reality:
Fire in the deep curves of your hair:
Your hips whirled in a tango,
Out and back in dim scented light;
Your cheeks snow-flushed, the zithers
Ringing, all the crowded ski lodge
Dancing and singing; your arms
White in the brown autumn water,
Swimming through the fallen leaves,

Making a fluctuant cobweb
Of light on the sycamores;
Your thigh's exact curve, the fine gauze
Slipping through my hands, and you
Tense on the verge of abandon;
Your breasts' very touch and smell;
The sweet secret odor of sex.
Forever the thought of you,
And the splendor of the iris,
The crinkled iris petal,
The gold hairs powdered with pollen,
And the obscure cantata
Of the tangled water, and the
Burning, impassive snow peaks,
Are knotted together here.
This moment of fact and vision
Seizes immortality,
Becomes the person of this place.
The responsibility
Of love realized and beauty
Seen burns in a burning angel
Real beyond flower or stone.

–KENNETH REXROTH, "INCARNATION"

On this new October day, in the year of our River Gods 1959, I have walked up a deep, shaded canyon through water, wet sand and golden redbud leaves. My feet are cold in boots and socks, yet the sun, low in its arc across the southwestern sky, keeps smiling through a sweet-smelling autumn haze.

When I find it, the slickrock bowl is creamed in gentle warmth.

After the brilliant, blazing heat of summer, the ambiance of this place has shifted considerably. Then, the bowl was like a sweaty exercise room; now, more like a balcony rimmed with the light from luminarias.

Boots and socks—off with them! The second my bare feet touch stone, I become a thermometer—the mercury moves past my toes, up through my legs and body to form a blush on my face—and what I see before me has already warmed my pulsing innards. This scooped-out place in an ancient dune of sand, turned to rock, has the look of a hammock, a cradle, a papyrus raft, or maybe Cleopatra's couch—anyhow, it's a tempting space, a space that invites me to lie down, roll over, stretch out, and feel the texture of time-beneath-the-elements that has formed this perfect sanctuary.

Yes, I've been here before. The first time, not alone—the other times, always. It's not that easy to find. We first came upon it by accident—a real accident—stumbled on the ridge and literally slipped, rolled and tumbled into this hollow to find ourselves unhurt, laughing . . . and completely alone. With no chance that anyone would be able to trace us, we stripped, slid into the pool at the lowest end of the bowl, came out dripping slick and made heady love skin-to-skin with the stone— same color as our own. I could feel the rock sucking at my back where we entwined above the pool, feel it against my body like warm silk—silkier than his, if you want to know—as if I were the center figure in a ménage a trois. And I know it was the slickrock that made that coupling a more memorable one.

I'm warm enough now in this nude place, to be the same; so I strip to my freckles and moles and walk down to the pothole, maybe to replay that fond memory as the water caresses me.

—KATIE LEE, "SANDSTONE SEDUCTION"

I must have been five years old, not much older. The grasses grew taller than my head, and all above me the thick blue sky stretched out like a tent. I watched a round bee wriggle into the pollen of sunflowers as if taking a bath. Far away my mother's voice called me in to dinner, while I dissolved into the sticky, insect-buzzing warmth of a late summer day in an English meadow.

Looking back, I believe that the soft grass of England was my first lover, teaching me that my body responds to a soft, slow touch, to vibrations of sound, to whispers on my skin—the tickling touch of stalks.

Yet how many of us place our bodies next to the Earth's anymore?

Sensuality is seeded in intimacy and thrives on proximity. We burrow into our mother's wombs, and later, wriggle and crawl over the ground, touching and tasting and smelling everything. To be in touch with our sensuality is to naturally bloom, to connect with the very spirit of creation. Life arises through contact; it thrives on familiarity and closeness, as do we.

–MARY REYNOLDS THOMPSON, FROM *RECLAIMING THE WILD SOUL*

Who knows at what moment
children lose their natural intimacy
with the animals and plants
of the earth, which
for a time
they share as equals?

When I was young,
my brother and I
used to swim in ponds
as warm as blood,
the color of tea,
and abounding with wildlife.

We floated like the frogs,
our legs trailing behind us,
and afterwards picked leeches
off each other
and lay in the sun.

I remember feeling the grass
growing up through my body
and my heart beating
down into the ground.

For a few enchanted summers,
we swam and basked
the afternoon away
while time stood still,
and the months from June
to September were measureless.

–SYDNEY EDDISON, "ENCHANTED SUMMERS"

The palms of my hands search for a pulse in the rocks. I continue walking. In some places my hips can barely fit through. I turn sideways, my chest and back in a vise of geologic time. I stop. The silence that lives in these sacred hallways presses against me. I relax. I surrender. I close my eyes. The arousal of my breath rises in me like music, like love, as the possessive muscles between my legs tighten and release. I come to the rock in a moment of stillness, giving and receiving, where there is no partition between my body and the body of Earth.

–TERRY TEMPEST WILLIAMS, FROM *DESERT QUARTET*

She's a big country. Her undulations
roll and flow in the sun. Those flanks
quiver when the wind caresses the grass.
Who turns away when so generous a body
offers to play hide-and-seek all summer?
One shoulder leans bare all the way up
the mountain; limbs range and plunge
wildly into the river. We risk our eyes
every day; they celebrate; they dance
and flirt over this offered treasure.
"Be alive," the land says. "Listen —
this is your time, your world, your pleasure."

–WILLIAM STAFFORD, "GODIVA COUNTY, MONTANA"
(WRITTEN 16 JUNE 1993, HIS LAST SUMMER)

These mountains sleep
side by side, nesting shoulder
along shoulder, knee behind knee,

asking for my hand to reach out
through this cabin window,

to reach toward the blue arc
of the hip, the green lift of the breast,
to lose my hand in the channels
of river, my fingers tickling in streams.

In this first light I can barely

call light, how the mist
rises from their curves, how their forms
quicken as I reach
toward them, how they reel in

breath when my hand brushes
trillium and fern, my fingertips
hush over moss. My hand flutters

like moth wing, like falling dogwood,
among the spring leaves
slips under the rocky ribs of creek
beds, ascends the explosion of rapids

in my cupped hand. Damp
and pungent, my hand returns to me,
fingers tracing my open lips

as these hills open to rain.

–Anita Skeen, "While You Sleep"

Their green flanks
and swells are not
flesh in any sense
matching ours,
we tell ourselves.
Nor their green breast nor their
green shoulder nor
the languor of their
rolling over.

–KAY RYAN, "GREEN HILLS"

There are dunes beyond Fish Springs. Secrets hidden from interstate travelers. They are the armatures of animals. Wind swirls around the sand and ribs appear. There is musculature in dunes.

And they are female. Sensuous curves — the small of a woman's back. Breasts. Buttocks. Hips and pelvis. They are the natural shapes of Earth. Let me lie naked and disappear.

–Terry Tempest Williams, from *Refuge*

During the day I laid out on a boulder. Took off my boots, socks, clothing. Unencumbered, I let the sun touch my skin. I washed my hair and let the sun dry it. The wind whipped it into long, lazy curls. Each strand took on a bit more sun each day until my hair was patinaed with gold. My skin burnished. At night sitting beneath the waxing moon, my skin held the warmth of the sun for hours. This is how I learned to catch and carry sun on my body and in my hair.

At full moon, against the faint persimmon moonlight reflected off the slickrock, once again I took off my clothes. Light fell around me. The wind began to sway the juniper branches. The shadows of boulders reached out to stroke me. I broke off sprigs of sage, crumbled them in my hands and rubbed sage over my body. I broke off several sprigs of juniper and plaited them in my hair. From my leather pouch I chose several pheasant feathers and wove them in with the juniper sprigs. I scooped up a handful of sienna-red earth and drew on my body: sun above one breast, moon above the other. Zigzag lightning on my arms. Spirals on my belly. I let the wind lead and I danced until moonset. Slowly each day thereafter, I let my skin fade until at new moon, it was time again to begin catching sun.

–P. K. PRICE, FROM "NAVIGATIONAL INFORMATION FOR SOLO FLIGHTS IN THE DESERT"

PROFUSION

The Church says: *The body is a sin.*
    Science says: *The body is a machine.*
    Advertising says: *The body is a business.*
    The body says: *I am a fiesta.*

–EDUARDO GALEANO, "WINDOW ON THE BODY"
(MARK FRIED TRANSLATION)

The power of love received in the body: This was the Festival!
   how we stood and faced one another
      and we took hands
      and the love came.
   And all the flowers swarmed about our heads:
      deep deep the sting goes.
Let love be welcomed the moment it seeks us.

–M. C. RICHARDS, FROM "PELTED BY BEAUTY"
(AFTER AN AMERICAN INDIAN FLOWER RITUAL)

That first summer, we went to her secret patch by the river. In the heat of late August, we picked two heaping buckets, then pelted each other with oozing fruit. She put blackberries on my tongue, and I painted her cheeks with purple juice. Back at her house, we made blackberry jam, the kettle steaming until the windows ran, and we slept holding each other's purple hands.

–CHARLES GOODRICH, FROM "WILD BLACKBERRIES"

The river in its abundance
many-voiced
all about us as we stood
on a warm rock to wash

slowly
smoothing in long
                sliding strokes
our soapy hands along each other's
slippery cool bodies

quiet and slow in the midst of
the quick of the
sounding river

our hands were flames
stealing upon quickened flesh until

no part of us but was
sleek and
on fire.

—DENISE LEVERTOV, "EROS AT TEMPLE STREAM"

66

The early summer light
steps birdlike
down the east slope of Green Mountain
and stirs low mists along the river
into flight.

Back inside, you lie
still asleep in your summer skin.
A blue sheet thrown back like a dress,
your dark hair
spilled rain over your shoulders.

Having so much and nothing at all
to say,
I slip cold arms around you.
You turn, sleepily,
and a deep green river
drifts away in your waking eyes.

From a wooden skiff
tied to a salmonberry bush,
you step ashore,
holding in your arms
everything I ever let slip away.

–TIM MCNULTY, "LITTLE RIVER LOVE POEM"

The snow will go for days, our road
keep trackless, and the lamplight
spill then stay. You're gold
in wool and overalls; you're a sight

to see: my man. One pear, one pound
of chestnuts in a paper bag, one kettle set
to burst. I'm smooth and round;
I'm a shallow bowl of oil: so sweet

for flame. Bring shovel, bring
salt and light a match to me—my bones
will melt. Honey, ring
me in garland: I'm a festival. Our home

is in the branches of jack pine. Our bedposts hum
like hives. Take this body. We'll make a wet thaw come.

–AUBREY RYAN, "O HONEY, WON'T YOU ROCK MY WORLD UP NORTH"

The Earth will be going on a long time
Before it finally freezes;
Men will be on it; they will take names,
Give their deeds reasons.
We will be here only
As chemical constituents —
A small franchise indeed.
Right now we have lives,
Corpuscles, Ambitions, Caresses,
Like everybody had once—

Here at the year's end, at the feast
Of birth, let us bring to each other
The gifts brought once west through deserts —
The precious metal of our mingled hair,
The frankincense of enraptured arms and legs,
The myrrh of desperate, invincible kisses —
Let us celebrate the daily
Recurrent nativity of love,
The endless epiphany of our fluent selves,
While the earth rolls away under us
Into unknown snows and summers,
Into untraveled spaces of the stars.

–KENNETH REXROTH, "LUTE MUSIC"

69

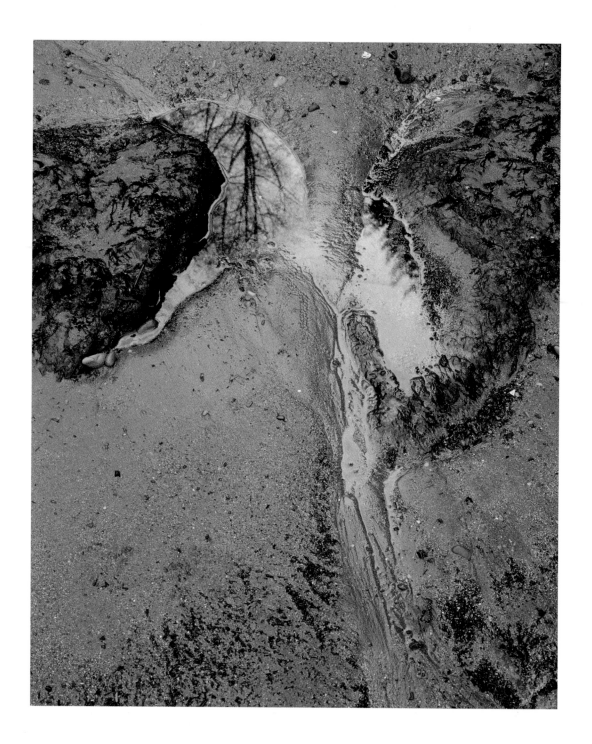

70

What is the body made of? The ancient elements. The same minerals we find in clay, in sand and mud, the stuff of earth. We share limbs, arms, and trunks with the trees. The dendrites of nerve cells and the bronchiole of the lung are both named for their resemblance to the branches of trees that extend in finer and finer lines from the central trunk, the main axis. Can you sense that your own spine is like a tree trunk, a ladder connecting ground and sky, heaven and earth? . . . or perhaps we are vertical rivers, walking watersheds, all our tissues supported by elaborate systems of irrigation and drainage. We are made of water and are thirsty for more. Water flows over the surface of the skin, the earth, across the land, on top of the land, inside the land, across the body, inside the body. . . . Fluid mysteries—water sings, and the body is the song.

–J. RUTH GENDLER, FROM *NOTES ON THE NEED FOR BEAUTY*

buried deep inside
stones sunk in the dark earth

these words sing in your bones
a song rising from the marrow

naming the places of your body
your body of lands and skies and seas

your lashes the naked spines of trees
sway in the winds of your waking eyes

your brow and cheeks summon the sun
your breath an invisible flight of birds

here is the rolling heartland of your breast
the sweeping plain of your abdomen

the tangled undergrowth of your groin
between the curved ridges of your hips

the well-spring of sweet waters flowing
into the sinuous rivers of your thighs

these are the things i sing
my tongue a troudabour of the flesh

traveling with its little drum
down the archipelago of your toes

–RANDY LUNDY, "BODY SONG"

Under everything, everything
a movement, slow as hair growth,
as the subtle click of cells turning
into other cells, the life in us
that grows as mountains grow.
Under everything this movement,
stars and wind circle around the smaller
circles of the grass, and the birds caged
in the kitchen sing it over and over,
inexplicably in their sweet chirps.

I feel it sometimes like today
somewhere in my torso, perhaps
sweet in the belly; this must be
what carrying a child is like.
I sit at a table and feel something
move with the pain of just before tears.
What is it the body says to me,
these tender aches that make me glad?
Not even one syllable is clear,
but if you were near I would tell you,
and you might lay your hand where the talking
starts and the pain, where my life
is still moving like an eaten live thing
and push your warmth into mine,
here, into the source of the singing.

–MARILYN NELSON, "THE SOURCE OF THE SINGING"

74

In the cedar grove, light shifted, and I dissolved backward, remembering a day on Knowles Creek, up the Siuslaw River from the Oregon coast. I stood ankle-deep in the water there to watch the caddis fly beginners fingering along over the rubbled streambed. They touched the stones where they walked hardly at all, buoyant and dancing along with a kind of tipsy assurance. Perhaps each held a bubble inside, to give its walk that jaunty ease. Many moved over the stones, their legs spidery with purpose.

I plucked one gently from the stream to study its self-made case: its coat, its house, burrow, cell? No word quite describes the sticky tube the caddis constructs about itself. With a twig I turned this one over in a bead of water on my thumb to list the makings of its cloak. First I recognized the stubby black of a hemlock needle, then the slate flakes of leaf, maybe year-old alder or maple, and a thread of moss, a tiny frond of something purple, dark pebbles of sand, a jewel of mica, some soggy filament which could be root, or a water-softened fiber of wood. It all fit together as the forest fit together. Knowles Creek tumbled about my feet, chilled numb, and I felt how my feet fit the round stones of that place better than any shoes.

As I squinted at the caddis in the gloom, my eyes resolved into focus beyond on a log by the stream. The loggers who worked the Knowles Creek drainage had left it somewhere upstream, the big butt swell of a hemlock or fir trunk, five feet through at the heavier upstream end, and twenty feet long. Still holding the recognizable shape of a log, it had softened inwardly to what we call a nurse log, a soggy bench better lit than soil, rot-softened and always wet. In deep forest, it is generally on the nurse log that a tree's seed, dormant through the winter, feels the sweet chemical tongue of water when spring warms it, and the tip of its embryo splits the seed case, turns down, chooses a place, and begins to lift a first green leaf.

I dipped my hand in the stream, the caddis walked away, careening past a mossy stone, and I splashed my numb feet across the stream to study the neighborhood of creatures harnessing the log, the small forest in a row.

The trunk lay thick, perhaps half a century dead where I put my hand on its damp flank. In its twenty-foot length, I counted what I could of that one log's population of greens and purples and reds: a clump of sword fern unfurling, wild iris blooming, fringe cup, thin-veined blackberry trailing down, the white bell blossoms of salal, the greenheart leaves of wild ginger popping up in a row, wild strawberry, five small hemlock trees with their bent heads swaying, a wand of cascara, one fir seedling knee-high, coast huckleberry with red fronds of furred new growth, Solomon's seal, tall and slender nettle, red huckleberry with its thin leaf circles of light, some small star-faced leaf I didn't know, inside-out flower, bunchberry, lacy grasses dusty with pollen, tiny cups rising from lichen, a whole small pantheon of mosses, and the thin leaves of rue. A solitary bee came humming down to enter a crevice, dressed in a blur of light. A long banana slug's calm progress left a shine. A cloud of gnats defined a favorable sphere of air. Two carpenter ants met, touched heads, went back the way they each had come, one up a fuzzy stem of thimbleberry, and the other into a neat round hole.

The caddis had walked the streambed, carrying its mosaic house, a miser of plain things. The log lay on the bank, a miser of creatures. The caddis held life inside, with a husk of debris. The log was dressed in a gown of life outside, with a core of inert punky wood. Each was a hull knit cleverly. The architecture of the forest begins with an accumulation of detail. The forest builds itself from the logic of this abundance, a teeming balance between the surge of growth and busy decay. In old-growth stands, a fallen log may seem more alive than a standing tree. This log by the stream shimmered. It lay like an ark carrying many lives forward past death into the next generation.

On the sun-warmed log, I lay on my belly among the mosses and felt the rush of its whole being, the entire purpose of the log and its citizens. The hum of sunlight spoke like a throb of music in the neighborhood on a hot night, when neither the children nor the grandmothers can contain their exuberance to be alive together. Insect buzz and blended flavors crowded about me. I touched my tongue to the moss and felt this rush in my own belly. I felt the green urge to make too many that is the urge that makes enough.

–KIM R. STAFFORD, "THE NURSE LOG'S CLOAK AND THE DWELLING OF CADDIS"

Lady of dusk-wood fastnesses,
      Thou art my Lady.
I have known the crisp, splintering leaf-tread with thee on before,
White, slender through green saplings;
I have lain by thee on the brown forest floor
      Beside thee, my Lady.

Lady of rivers strewn with stones,
      Only thou art my Lady.
Where thousand the freshets are crowded like peasants to a fair;
Clear-skinned, wild from seclusion
They jostle white-armed down the tent-bordered thoroughfare
      Praising my Lady.

–WILLIAM CARLOS WILLIAMS, "FIRST PRAISE"

In a rainforest, it rains. But the rain doesn't just fall to the ground, soak into soil. It covers everything. It clings so completely that, even after the rain stops falling from the sky, even when the sun has shone all day, it still rains. On me. As I walk through it. The trail is spongy with sphagnum moss and my feet get wet. Even the driftwood planks laid across the muddiest spots are wet, and I slip on mossy wood. Skunk cabbage, as big as my three-year-old son and studded with diamonds of rain, slap my legs, spraying water. Slender grasses, green orchid, purple aster, and ladies tresses shiver as I pass, releasing more liquid. This rain is like seed that disperses by attaching to a passing animal's fur, so easily do I gather rain to my body. Droplets seem to jump onto me, as if dry is simply an abstract concept here, as if an equilibrium of wet on all things must be maintained. Onward. I scramble up a hill, grabbing onto roots. Now salmonberry and blueberry wave wet against my hips. Spruce and hemlock saplings rub my shoulders and pat my back with wet needles. A passing breeze coats my hair and face in the life-blood of this forest. If I stay here long enough, will the hair on my arms grow moss? Will tendrils of Old Man's beard hang around my face? Will my feet sink even deeper into black soil until I am rooted in place?

–MARYBETH HOLLEMAN, FROM *THE HEART OF THE SOUND*

The fern in the rain breathes the silver message.
Stay, lie low. Play your dark reeds
and relearn the beauty of absorption.
There is nothing beyond the rotten log
covered with leaves and needles.
Forget the light emerging with its golden wick.
Raise your face to the water-laden frond.
A thousand blossoms will fall into your arms.

—ANNE CORAY, "THE ART OF BEING"

We may need to be cured by flowers.

   We may need to strip naked and let the petals fall on our shoulders, down our bellies, against our thighs. We may need to lie naked in fields of wildflowers. We may need to walk naked through beauty. We may need to walk naked through color. We may need to walk naked through scent. We may need to walk naked through sex and death. We may need to feel beauty on our skin. We may need to walk the pollen path, among the flowers that are everywhere.

—SHARMAN APT RUSSELL, FROM *ANATOMY OF A ROSE*

you are so full of wonders
that I will remember you
in my next life

that when I come back again
as an apple tree
I will devote
a whole year's growth to you

you will be apples

from winter sleep
to blossom
to bud
to summer leaves
to ripe fruit falling
on autumnal ground

feeding bird
and beetle
earth
and tree

–JOE PULICHINO, "LOVE SONG FOR ALL"

My words rained over you, stroking you.
A long time I have loved the sunned mother-of-pearl of your body.
I go so far as to think that you own the universe.
I will bring you happy flowers from the mountains, bluebells,
dark hazels, and rustic baskets of kisses.
I want to do with you what spring does with the cherry trees.

–PABLO NERUDA, FROM "EVERY DAY YOU PLAY" (W. S. MERWIN TRANSLATION)

From blossoms comes
this brown paper bag of peaches
we bought from the boy
at the bend in the road where we turned toward
signs painted Peaches.

From laden boughs, from hands,
from sweet fellowship in the bins,
comes nectar at the roadside, succulent
peaches we devour, dusty skin and all,
comes the familiar dust of summer, dust we eat.

O, to take what we love inside,
to carry within us an orchard, to eat
not only the skin, but the shade,
not only the sugar, but the days, to hold
the fruit in our hands, adore it, then bite into
the round jubilance of peach.

There are days we live
as if death were nowhere
in the background; from joy
to joy to joy, from wing to wing,
from blossom to blossom to
impossible blossom, to sweet impossible blossom.

—Li-Young Lee, "From Blossoms"

Lying beside you I hear the wind
combing the trees of distant mountains
far from these arid arguments
in which we wander, love's nomads,
pitching and breaking our frail camps
on the contours of mood and intent.

I smell that green lake where salamanders
break the surface to silver fans
with their prehensile twist and dip.
We are not so distant in our sliding
across the faces of our needs,
searching for those lulls when,
through a silence deeper than sleep,
all we are windows itself at once
and we see with the body's lucid eyes
past personality's mutable weather.

Your lips comb the forests of my thighs.
Between sloped walls of flesh your breath
clouds over us like mountain steam.
For you, now, I would disown those diamonds
embedded in the dark coal of common sense,
would give you my belly like a meadow,
call you like a deer to browse.

I give my body to the compass of your hands,
reveal in a voice cracked as the raven's
that wilderness under my skin,
blood rivers coursing their red canyons,
arroyos and dusky plateaus.
You are the stone, the rod, and the serpent.
I am that river springing out of a stone,
irrigating these deserts of night,
scattering armfuls of roses.

–CAROL JANE BANGS, "LOVE AFTER ANGER"

COMMUNION

The rhythm of the cosmos is something we cannot get away from, without bitterly impoverishing our lives. . . . We *must* get back into relation, vivid and nourishing relation to the cosmos and the universe. The way is through daily ritual, and the reawakening. We *must* once more practise the ritual of dawn and noon and sunset, the ritual of the kindling fire and pouring water, the ritual of the first breath, and the last. . . . the ritual of the moon in her phases. . . . the ritual of the seasons. . . . the togetherness of the body, the sex, the emotions, the passions, with the earth and sun and stars.

–D. H. LAWRENCE, FROM *A PROPOS OF "LADY CHATTERLEY'S LOVER"*

Body and land are one flesh. They are made of the same stuff. Their beauty is one beauty, their wounds the same wounds. They call to us in the same perennial voice, crying, Come see, come touch, come listen and smell, and O come taste. We explore them alike, honor or abuse them alike. The health or sickness of one is inseparable from that of the other. There is no division between where we live and what we are. . . .

We think of sex too narrowly, as though it were a mere magnetism of groin to groin. The sensuous attraction that pulls us into bed is a special case of the greater attraction that binds us, nerves and belly and brain, to the flesh of the earth.

–SCOTT RUSSELL SANDERS, FROM "EARTH'S BODY"

94

To be in relation to everything around us, above us, below us, earth, sky, bones, blood, flesh, is to see the world whole, even holy. . . . The lightning we witness crack and charge a night sky in the desert is the same electricity we feel in ourselves whenever we dare to touch flesh, rock, body, and earth.

–Terry Tempest Williams, from "The Erotic Landscape"

Why is it that we often feel a connection while gazing at the stars? Our bodies contain hydrogen, carbon, and oxygen—elements that came from the Big Bang that created the universe between ten and twenty billions years ago. We are, in fact, stardust that sifted down into the ocean, morphed, and eventually crawled out of that churning cauldron. At night from my campsite in the saguaros, I watch the stars emerge like a million eyes and ponder where we came from. Meteorites sail by to the east over the Ajos, leaving long green trails as they go.

–Carol Ann Bassett, from *Organ Pipe: Life on the Edge*

Some nights I visit the mountains,
called by the voice of the wind
fluting through old growth forests,

and I find myself lying on the lip
of a cliff, the night sky wedding me
to stone, stars falling through me.

Some nights I lie there till dawn,
becoming something other—some
elemental animal of fire whose

memories flare and go out, leaving
me like ashes that will wash down
the rock face to earth.

Some say I only dream these
mountains, that they are not real,
and no beast born of fire can live.

I tell them I have been there,
that the cliff bears the mold of
my face, and that my flesh still

smolders with the light of dying
stars, though it does not hurt to
burn my way back home.

–PENNY HARTER, "SOME NIGHTS"

98

We were to have late-afternoon tea on Fifth Avenue, at The Pierre, one of Manhattan's classiest hotels, which serves its clientele in one of the city's foremost tea rooms. We had been there before and knew that afternoon tea, and the sweets that came with it, required a kind of invisible, feminine way of eating, eating accomplished while speaking quietly, mysteriously, hushed, all proper and English-like, frosted with the air kisses of the French. We knew to expect classical music, to sit where we had sat before, in overstuffed tapestry-upholstered chairs, our legs daintily crossed, our bodies drenched by small clouds of smoke blown by rich ladies lunching. We would finger delicate sandwiches of cucumber and cream cheese, and colorful cookies and brownies and Belgian chocolates. These were the offerings we would make to our bodies, once we arrived.

But outside, on the windy streets, the orange sky of late October flung itself into dark corridors of the city, and into me, as I made my way to The Pierre. So though my friend was beautiful, walking to the corner to meet me, her hair a wild breeze of black curls, her loose paisley pants flowing like water down her legs, her shoulders warm inside a thick blue wool sweater, I knew I could not go for tea. When she stood beside me, smelling like a vase of apple cider, cinnamon, and lingering chimney smoke, all I could imagine was tilting our heads toward the falling sun and spilling our hair into leaves dropping in Central Park.

It was about this time we began listening to the deeper stirrings of our bodies. Believing our fingers had a feeling for dangling through grass in Central Park's Great Lawn; believing our lungs could lure us to the cherry air blossoming around the reservoir; believing our spines ached to arch along the ancient gray boulders near Sheep Meadow; believing in the sparrow's music by the boat pond. In a city of wealthy and fancy kingdoms, we had inherited these smaller, richer delights of Central Park.

This is how, months later, we approached a threshold: the decision to cross the park's frozen lake one winter day, before we married our men and had our children. There was the scattering snow, like breathlessness, the rupturing wind, a lucid sky. We could love this. Now, still, we talk of that day, when the ghosts of our girlness led us across the ice and into virgin snow, where we spread our limbs in the powder and drew upon the earth our angels trapped inside. We, women, urban women, fell to the ground, silent, and swallowed the wet, cold earth that raised us, the sweet earth we otherwise might never again have tasted.

–LISA COUTURIER, "SNOW DAY"

To either side, heat wavers
across the fields, skimming tops of wheat
just beginning to flower. Farther on,

morning glories choke the corn
and white grubs turn unseen at the root.

In this season, you can lose
children deep in the two-mile rows.

Early evening, I stop my truck
by our north field, step out,
and lie down in the thick border grass

in the sweet seedy heat
with summer humming. High above

Taurus keeps his head down
as he crosses the sky,
slow and powerful in his dumb resolve.

–CAROL WESTBERG, "NOT GETTING THERE"

From the hungry gnaw that eats me night and day,
From native moments, from bashful pains, singing them,
Seeking something yet unfound though I have diligently sought it many a long year,
Singing the true song of the soul fitful at random,
Renascent with grossest Nature or among animals,
Of that, of them and what goes with them my poems informing,
Of the smell of apples and lemons, of the pairing of birds,
Of the wet of woods, of the lapping of waves,
Of the mad pushes of waves upon the land, I them chanting,
The overture lightly sounding, the strain anticipating,
The welcome nearness, the sight of the perfect body,
The swimmer swimming naked in the bath, or motionless on his back
      lying and floating,
The female form approaching, I pensive, love-flesh tremulous aching,
The divine list for myself or you or for any one making,
The face, the limbs, the index from head to foot, and what it arouses,
The mystic deliria, the madness amorous, the utter abandonment,
(Hark close and still what I now whisper to you,
I love you, O you entirely possess me,
O that you and I escape from the rest and go utterly off, free and lawless,
Two hawks in the air, two fishes swimming in the sea not more lawless than we;)
The furious storm through me careering, I passionately trembling.

—WALT WHITMAN, FROM "FROM PENT-UP ACHING RIVERS"

Now the sun rides bareback
on our necks again,
returning us to the colors of cockscomb,
ruffling the fields in rows of gladness
after summer rain,

now the tomatoes
fill us with gladness,
basil splays its spicy anise-
perfumed leaves for us;

peaches break apart
in our hands,
each half an aureole of sweetness;
purple figs ooze gladness
from their purple rumps;
the cream swirls in our coffee
like a cirrus cloud.

And while the birds cut open
the vast plains of sky
with the dark scissors of their wings,

while the birds sew shut the sky
with the dark-feathered needles
of their wings,

we have the drying but still green
grass tangled through my fingers
like your hair,
we have your hair between my fingers
black and soft as grief,

we have the narrow stream,
the bottom-loving carp,
the orange of their tails and fins —

we have this breeze
like a dream of a breeze,
we have my dress pulled up,
my bare and heated thighs.

–RUTH L. SCHWARTZ, "PICNIC"

Our sense of self, society, and spirituality are inseparably linked to our sexuality. The world is driven by two opposite streams of energy in constant intercourse. To and fro, the motion of copulation is the heartbeat of reality. The universe, from the heavens to atoms, is sexual. Men and women, through the ecstatic state of sexual orgasm, stand poised in a harmony of these opposites: it is our deepest contact with the balance of nature and the origins of existence.

–ROBERT LAWLOR, FROM *EARTH HONORING: THE NEW MALE SEXUALITY*

He watched her face, and her eyes never shifted; they were with him while she moved out of her clothes and while she slipped his jeans down his legs, stroking his thighs. She unbuttoned his shirt, and all he was aware of was the heat of his own breathing and the warmth radiating from his belly, pulsing between his legs. He was afraid of being lost, so he repeated trail marks to himself: this is my mouth tasting the salt of her brown breasts; this is my voice calling out to her. He eased himself deeper within her and felt the warmth close around him like river sand, softly giving way under foot, then closing firmly around the ankle in cloudy warm water. But he did not get lost, and he smiled at her as she held his hips and pulled him closer. He let the motion carry him, and he could feel the momentum within, at first almost imperceptible, gathering in his belly. When it came, it was the edge of a steep riverbank crumbling under the downpour until suddenly it all broke loose and collapsed into itself.

–LESLIE MARMON SILKO, FROM CEREMONY

When you enter me,
I am black soil
rich with the humus
of ancestral bones
tilled smooth.

Breathing dust from your beard,
your hay-strewn hair,
I lick your skin
grateful for hard labor,
for all we plant
together, for sweat,
for the flavor of earth.

–LINDA M. HASSELSTROM, "BENEDICTION FOR SWEAT"

She sits naked on a rock
a few yards out in the water.
He stands on the shore,
also naked, picking blueberries.
She calls. He turns. She opens
her legs showing him her great beauty,
and smiles, a bow of lips
seeming to tie together
the ends of the earth.
Splashing her image
to pieces, he wades out
and stands before her, sunk
to the anklebones in leaf-mush
and bottom-slime—the intimacy
of the visible world. He puts
a berry in its shirt
of mist into her mouth.
She swallows it. He puts in another.
She swallows it. Over the lake
two swallows whim, juke, jink,
and when one snatches
an insect they both whirl up
and exult. He is swollen
not with ichor but with blood.
She takes him and sucks him
more swollen. He kneels, opens
the dark, vertical smile
linking heaven with the underearth

and licks her smoothest flesh more smooth.
On top of the rock they join.
Somewhere a frog moans, a crow screams.
The hair of their bodies
startles up. They cry
in the tongue of the last gods,
who refused to go,
chose death, and shuddered
in joy and shattered in pieces,
bequeathing their cries
into the human mouth. Now in the lake
two faces float, looking up
at a great maternal pine whose branches
open out in all directions
explaining everything.

–GALWAY KINNELL, "LAST GODS"

I   will   be   earth   you   be   the   flower
You   have   found   my   root   you   are   the   rain
I   will   be   boat   and   you   the   rower
You   rock   you   toss   me   you   are   the   sea
How   be   steady   earth   that's   now   a   flood
The   root's   the   oar's   afloat   where's   blown   our   bud
We   will   be   desert   pure   salt   the   seed
Burn   radiant   sex   born   scorpion   need

—MAY SWENSON, "UNTITLED"

The room is a conch shell
and echoing in it, the blood
rushes in the ears,
the surf of desire sliding in
on the warm beach.

The room is the shell of the moon
snail, gorgeous predator
whose shell winds round and round
the color of moonshine
on your pumping back.

The bed is a slipper shell
on which we rock, opaline
and pearled with light sweat,
two great deep currents
colliding into white water.

The clam shell opens.
The oyster is eaten.
The squid shoots its white ink.
Now there is nothing but warm
salt puddles on the flats.

—Marge Piercy, "Salt in the Afternoon"

Here, we are one geography:
every part of us inked on a map
where, across all the blue waters,
continents' edges inexplicably match.

I move closer to you in the dark,
feel the slow heat
that embers you deeper into the night.
Where all fires descend a few hours
into their own slow-dreaming hearts.
Where the ravine hides in its own steepness
no matter how long, how fiercely we love.

–JANE HIRSHFIELD, "SLEEPING"

Build a house in a gorge where mountains meet.
People together are as powerful as the sacred place

Where two rivers become one waterway.
In that place the chi is strong, the people resilient.

Practice the riverhead and the calm, abiding pool.
Practice the sacred air, let the breath grow shallow,

Soft, even cease to be. Let Timelessness blossom in you.
Take the hills as effortlessly as you cross a room.

Meet at the Dragon Points. Gather at the Celestial Gate.
Turn the key.

–ROBERT MCDOWELL, "IN THE FOREST"

The longer I live here on earth, the more I love the light of sunrise, the silent tumble of snow from motionless branch, mute raven's track in mud, moonset at dawn over a field of silky grasses, sleeping cows, spiders, thin trickling of the world's water.

Now, after all these years, I'm becoming literate in the other language. My feet know the twist of knobby spruce roots. My hands caress soft moss beds. I've smelled leaf mold on autumn mist, tasted sun-hot blueberries. And occasionally, as I touch, taste, and listen, the boundary between nature and me becomes a threshold: I step across. The wild either slips into me, or comes leaping up, like a silver fish, flashing out of my own dark wildness.

–BETH POWNING, FROM HOME: CHRONICLE OF A NORTH COUNTRY LIFE

Listen.
Below us.
Above us.
Inside us.
Come.
This is all there is.

–TERRY TEMPEST WILLIAMS, FROM *DESERT QUARTET*

ACKNOWLEDGMENTS

FROM LORRAINE:

I give thanks to Sheridan McCarthy, who connected me with Mary Reynolds Thompson and thence to White Cloud Press. Thanks to Steve Scholl and Christy Collins for understanding my vision and helping bring it to beautiful fruition. I'm deeply grateful to the members of my writing group, who gave moral support and helpful feedback on many aspects of the book during its long, slow gestation: Carla Wise, Carol Savonen, and Lee Sherman. And to my tribe of Indiegogo supporters, whose generosity is the wind beneath my wings: Cleve Anderson and Lynn Scalzi, Diana Blakney, James Bombardier, Martha Bracken, Karyle Butcher, Jack Compere and Marvel Vigil, Sydney Eddison, Beeara Edmonds and Russ Phillips, the Rex Flash Ministries, Annie Folger, Madeleine Grant, Lisa Grinnell, Anna Joy Thigpen Hunt, Victoria Hutchinson, Annette Mills and David Eckert, Kirk and Susan Nevin, Lynne Nittler, Rick Palkovic, Bob and Laura Peckyno, Jack Peterson, Pauline Presson, Caroline Rose, Mia Schroer, Claudia Schulz, Suzanne Shaw, Lee Sherman, Scott Slovic and Susie Bender, Jean Troy Smith, Diane Steele, Virginia Thigpen, Patti Warner, Rebecca Warner, Elizabeth Weal, Miriam Wells, Stephen Westfold, Kathy Williams, Beth Young, and many others.

FROM BRUCE:

I'd like to thank first and foremost Elizabeth Weal, who's consistently provided love, support, and inspiration for my photographic adventures. Thanks also to my daughters, Chelsea and Caroline, for their enthusiasm and patience. I'd like to especially thank three photographers who helped propel and sustain me on my photographic journey: Charles Cramer, Marion Patterson, and David Hibbard. Thanks also go to Adam Stern, Tia Rich, and Virginia Stern for exhibition karma. Finally, I'd like to thank the many people who have appreciated my work over the years.

SOURCES

LIST OF PHOTOGRAPHS

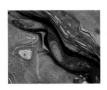

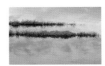

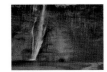

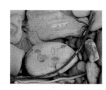

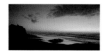
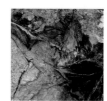

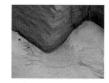

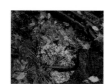

INDEX OF AUTHORS AND TITLES

LORRAINE ANDERSON grew up on a chicken ranch in the Santa Clara Valley of California in the days when it was still known as the Valley of Heart's Delight, when blossoming orchards stretched in springtime as far as the eye could see. She contains the imprint of the earth's beauty in her cells. With a bachelor's degree in English from the University of Utah and a master's degree in creation spirituality with an emphasis in ecopsychology from Naropa University, she became certified as a yoga teacher in 2013. She edited *Sisters of the Earth: Women's Prose and Poetry about Nature* (1991, 2003); co-edited *Wild in the Willamette* (with Abby Phillips Metzger, 2015), *Literature and the Environment: A Reader on Nature and Culture* (with Scott Slovic and John O'Grady, 1998, 2012), and *At Home on This Earth: Two Centuries of U.S. Women's Nature Writing* (with Tom Edwards, 2002); and co-authored *Cooking with Sunshine* (with Rick Palkovic, 2006).

BRUCE HODGE is a fine art photographer who has exhibited at various venues around the San Francisco Bay Area, where he has lived since 1979. His most recent show was by invitation at the American Association for the Advancement of Science in Washington, DC. In addition to his work as a photographer, Hodge is a computer scientist currently employed by Adobe Systems, a leader in the production of software for the visual arts industry, and is the founder of Carbon-Free Palo Alto (http://carbonfreepaloalto. org). He names Brett and Edward Weston, Wynn Bullock, and Minor White as photographers who have influenced his work. Hodge writes, "One of my challenges is to become unbound from my own concepts of nature and its reality and to release my senses to the world around me." He recently produced a limited edition of hand printed "portfolio" books that feature a selection of his images (http://tenaya.com).

ROBERT MICHAEL PYLE founded the Xerces Society for Invertebrate Conservation in 1971 while studying butterfly conservation as a Fulbright Scholar in England. He holds a Ph.D. in butterfly eco-geography from Yale University. His eighteen books include *Wintergreen, The Butterflies of Cascadia, Chasing Monarchs, Mariposa Road,* and *Evolution of the Genus Iris: Poems.*